301

WRITING
IDEAS

chartwell
books

CALLING ALL WRITERS!

The written word—it is a primary form of communication for everyday life. From directional street signs to instruction manuals, it guides us through the most mundane yet necessary actions. Words and text teach us and keep us safe. Writing things down helps us with retention and memory. It has been said that if you are a good writer, a good communicator of whatever point is trying to be articulated, then you can work anywhere. Across every business industry, good comprehension and writing ability is a valued skill.

But outside of the practical, words and the act of writing are also deeply personal and intimate forms of expression. Writing down what you think and feel is an act of self-care. When you let words flow out of you onto paper or the screen, you no longer have to hold them inside your body, heart, and mind, thus releasing any tension, stress, or bad feelings associated with them. Likewise, if you are

301

WRITING
IDEAS

happy, excited, or passionate about a cause, writing about it will help you feel refreshed and energized. All in all, writing is extremely cathartic.

The prompts that follow here are designed to motivate you to dig deep and ask questions you might never think to answer. These are writing exercises—they work out your creative muscles and push your mind and imagination to the limits. Some of them might even cause you to do some research around certain topics, thus expanding your worldview and general knowledge.

Anyone can write, and the best way to start writing is to START WRITING. Just pick up a pen, pencil, crayon, quill, or laptop and begin.

Happy writing!

1. What is a day that you wish you could relive?

2. Describe the day you graduated high school.

3. How did you picture your life in the future as a child?

----

4. Write about a place that you go to be alone.

----

5. When was the last time you received exciting news?

6. What do you do to get your mind off things when you're stressed?

7. Write about the last time someone asked you to
keep a secret.

9. Write about a piece of clothing you have owned at any
point in your life. What about it stands out?

8. Describe an opinion you have that has changed since you were a child.

10. Write about your first kiss. Who was it with?

11. Write about the first time you fell in love.

12. Describe a moment in time that you had wished
you could disappear.

13. What was the last thing that made you cry?

14. Do you feel fulfilled by your work? Why or why not?

15. Write about the best relationship you have ever experienced. (Does not have to be romantic).

16. Write about someone who had an impact on your life.

17. Write about a song that reminds you of a time from childhood.

18. Write about a time in which you helped someone that you did not have to.

19. If I looked under your bed, what would I find?

20. Write about a vacation you took as a child.

21. Write about the most memorable vacation you've ever taken. What sticks out about it that makes it special?

22. If you could travel anywhere in the world, where would you go?

23. What was the first meal you learned to cook?

24. Write about your favorite food. When was the first time you tried it?

25. Finish the phrase, "The early bird gets…"

26. What animal do you think best represents your personality?

27. Write about your favorite TV show.

28. Write a one-minute apology letter.

29. Write about a decision you've made that you would change if you could go back in time.

30. Describe a piece of furniture in your home that says something about who you are.

31. Do you believe in an afterlife?

32. Write about a time you did something spontaneous.

33. Describe a time that you learned a valuable lesson.

34. If you could change something about yourself,
physically or in terms of personality, what would it be?

35. Do you have or like tattoos? What do tattoos say
about a person?

36. Is religion an important factor in choosing your partner/spouse?

37. Do you believe in marriage?

38. Describe something you have built.

39. What do you consider to be your greatest accomplishment?

40. If you could be a celebrity, what would you want to be famous for?

41. Where do you think the most clearly?

42. Write about someone you have lost contact with. What would you say if you bumped into them?

43. Has there ever been a time that you felt left out? Describe how this made you feel in detail.

44. If you could remain one age forever, what would it be?

45. What weather forecast would best represent how
you feel today?

46. What kind of cake do you prefer on your birthday?

47. What is your earliest memory?

48. Write about a time you knowingly lied. Do you regret it?

49. Write about your first experience with death.

50. What is your opinion of cloning humans?

51. Do you believe communism can work in practice?

52. Write about your most serious injury. How old were you
when it happened?

53. What is the hardest part of your daily life?

54. Are there any traditions you inherited from your parents? Do you keep them?

55. What is your favorite season? Why?

56. How do you reward yourself after a difficult day?

57. After a terrible day, who would be your first choice to talk to about it?

58. There is going to be a movie produced in which you are the main character. What is the title and what actor should play you?

59. Imagine you are a farmer. What do you grow?

60. Write about a time you saw something you wish
you hadn't seen.
61. Should people be given second chances?

62. Do you believe in the death penalty?

63. Have you ever had an idea for an invention? If so, what was it?

64. What are your favorite activities for a rainy day?

65. What is your greatest fear? Have you ever experienced it?

66. Imagine you are a taxi driver. What city would you like your taxi to be in?

67. Are there such things as soulmates? If yes, have you met yours?

68. What is the funniest joke you know?

69. Write about a time you felt deeply jealous?

70. What is the right age to retire? What do you hope for your retirement?

71. Should Earth consider colonizing Mars?

72. What was the hardest choice you have ever had to make?

73. Write about a coincidence that ended up changing the course of your life.

74. Can there be both destiny and free will? If not, which do you believe to be true?

75. What is something you wish you had done as a child?

76. Write about a large argument you've had. Would you say anything different if you could relive it?

77. Write about your favorite book. Why is it special?

78. If you were a household object, what would you be?

79. Of all your dreams, which sticks out to you as the most memorable? Was it a good dream or a nightmare?

80. If you were a playing card, what kind of card would you be? Would you be a specific suit?

81. What is the best gift you have ever received? Who gave it to you?

82. Do you believe in superstitions? If so, what are some
superstitions you have? If not, why do you think people
believe them?

83. Do you sometimes wish you could switch life positions with someone specific? If so, who would it be?

84. Describe someone you wish you had never met.

85. Is there somewhere you would never go?

86. Write about the most beautiful place you have ever been to. What were you doing there and who were you with?

87. What is something that you wish was less expensive?

88. Would you rather travel by public transportation
or by car?

89. Write about a person you just met.

90. Is it possible to know everything about a person by looking at them?

91. Imagine you were an advertiser in charge of selling a bar of soap. Describe a commercial for the soap and write a catchy slogan.

92. Did you have a celebrity crush as child? If so, who was it? Would you go on a date with them now?

93. What is something that you fear you will never get to experience?

94. What is the most beautiful piece of art you have ever seen? Where did you see it? How did it make you feel?

95. If you were an ice cream flavor what would you be?

96. If I looked in your refrigerator right now, what are three things that I would see?

97. If you had to hide in your house, where is the first place you would go?

98. Write about your scariest experience in a car.

99. If you could have any superpower, what would it be?

100. Do you think there is life on another planet? If so, do you think it has visited Earth?

101. If you could time travel, what era of history would you live in? Why?

102. What is more important, physical, or spiritual gain?

103. Do you think social media has improved or worsened modern life?

104. Write about something that you wish you did less.

105. Imagine there is a storm and your power cuts out.
Describe how you would handle this situation.

106. What is your favorite memory in the snow?

107. Has there ever been a time that you felt betrayed?
Describe the situation and what you would have
done differently.

108. Write about a time that you felt ill. What comforts
you most when you feel sick?

109. If commercial space travel were possible, but the
shortest allowed trip was two years, would you do it?
If so, where would you go?

110. Write about the three most important qualities you
search for in a partner.

111. Do you think it is important to have a morning routine? If so, what is yours?

112. Write about the last time you felt exhilarated. What were you doing and who were you with?

113. Write about a time that you bought something expensive that you ended up regretting. How old were you and why did you buy it?

114. Can money buy love? Why or why not?

115. What is something you think everyone should experience at least once in life?

116. Do you believe that we have become too dependent on technology as a society? Why or why not?

117. What about your parents defines who you are and what you do?

_____

_____

_____

_____

_____

_____

_____

_____

_____

118. Write about the first time you felt like an adult.

_____

_____

_____

_____

_____

_____

_____

_____

_____

_____

119. What is something that you miss about being a child?

120. Imagine you are a sailor lost at sea with one other person. There is enough food left to feed one person for three days. Describe your course of action.

121. Should all public college be free? Why or why not?

122. Write about a time that you were lost. Where were you going and how did you find your way?

123. Describe a time you felt trapped, (physically or psychologically), and how you handled the situation.

124. What has been the worst choice you have made in life and why? How would your life be different if you had chosen differently?

125. Is having children a necessary part of life? If so, when is the perfect age and why?

126. Write about something that you often forget to do.

127. Write about a time that you idealized something. What was it and how has your opinion shifted?

128. Imagine you are interviewing for a job and someone asks you to describe yourself in two words. Which words would choose and why?

129. Imagine you are on death row. What would you choose to be your final meal and why?

130. There is a phrase that states, "An eye for an eye." Come up with a new ending to the phrase beginning "An eye for…"

131. Write about someone in your life that irritates you. What about them is so frustrating?

132. Write about a time you saw someone for the last time without knowing you would never see them again. Would you say something different if you could go back in time?

133. Some people say the "eyes are windows to the soul".
Do you agree with this, why or why not?

134. What is the most important amenity for any
hotel to contain?

135. Have you ever taken a road trip? If so describe where you went and who you were with. If not, write about where you would want to go and who you would want to take.

136. How important are first impressions? What is the first thing you typically notice about someone?

137. Describe your favorite restaurant. What type of food is it? Is there something specific that makes it unique?

138. Write about the last time that you wrote a letter to someone. Who was it addressed to and what was it about?

139. Do letters have more value in personal communication than emails?

140. Write about the most expensive meal you have ever eaten. When was it and who were you with? Was it worth the price?

141. Do you believe in the practice of meditation? If so, is it something you have ever done before?

142. Is there something or someone that you could not live without? If so, what or who is it?

143. Imagine you were just informed that you won the lottery. Who is the first person you would call and what is the first thing you would buy?

144. What invention has had the greatest impact on modern society?

145. Using your five senses, describe a warm summer night.

146. Is hate or love a more powerful motivator?

147. Write about a time that you pitied someone.

148. Have you ever had an outer body experience? If yes, describe it in detail.

149. Do your past experiences have to shape who you are as a person today?

150. Write about a time that you hid something from someone you loved.

151. Describe three animals that you have seen recently.

152. Write about the ocean and describe your most memorable experience with the ocean. What do you remember seeing, smelling, hearing, or feeling?

153. Describe the most memorable photograph you have ever taken or been in. Where were you and what were you doing?

154. Write about an experience you had on an airplane.
Describe in detail everything that you heard and saw.

155. Describe a time going through airport security. Write about how you felt and what you thought about.

156. Imagine you are a mannequin in a department store. Write about everything you experience.

157. Write about an experience you have had at the doctor's office. Describe how you felt and why this experience stands out to you.

158. Write about a challenge that you overcame. Describe what it took to overcome it.

159. Has there ever been a time that you doubted yourself?
If yes, write about your experience. If no, describe
weather or not you believe this has helped you or hurt you
in life.

160. How important is outward confidence, even if someone is unsure of their decision?

161. Write about a time that you pretended to be someone
else, literally or metaphorically.

162. Write about a time that you did badly on a test.
Describe how you felt in detail.

163. Are standardized tests an accurate reflection of someone's intelligence?

164. Write about something you wish your parents had done differently as you grew up. How do you think this would have changed who you are today?

165. Write about a skill you possess that few people are aware of.

166. Write about a time that you regretted a decision.
Describe the emotions you felt and why you felt this way.

167. What is one major difference between your childhood and that of those growing up today?

168. Should all children be made to wear uniforms at school?

169. Write about a time that you looked at the stars. Where were you and how did you feel?

170. Imagine that space travel has become easily accessible and you have been tasked with writing a short advertisement recruiting people to travel to space. Include persuasive language in your advertisement.

171. Do you prefer cats, dogs, or neither? Explain your preference.

172. Write about the last time that you felt competitive.
Did you succeed in what you were doing?

173. Write about a time that you were in or around a hospital. What did you see and how did you feel in the moment?

174. Describe someone that you have a deep respect for. How did they earn this respect?

175. Write about an experience you had receiving
help from a stranger.

176. Write about a time that you got punished as a child.
Looking back, was the punishment justified?

177. Write about someone or something that intimidates you.
Describe this person or thing in detail.

178. Describe a time that you did something outside of your comfort zone. Were you happy you did it afterward?

179. Are zoos ethical? Write about an experience you have had visiting a zoo and how it made you feel.

180. Do you prefer living in the country or city? Explain your reasoning.

181. Write about a time that you accidently broke
something. Describe how you felt and the repercussions you
faced for breaking it.

182. What does it mean to be a genius? Describe someone who
you believe meets this standard.

183. Describe something socially accepted that you wish would change.

184. Write about a time you lost something whether it be an object, a feeling, or a person. How did this make you feel and how did you recover?

185. Write a short paragraph of advice to someone who has recently had their heart broken.
186. Write about a time that you were persuaded to do something.

187. Pretend you are involved in the creation of a time capsule. Describe three objects that you would pick to put in it to be saved for future generations as a representation of today.

188. Write about an experience you have had at the dentist.

189. Is it important to do what you love as a job? Why or why not?

190. Write about a memorable family gathering from your childhood. Who and what specifically sticks out about it?

191. Write about a time that you awkwardly said something you shouldn't have. Who were you with and what did you say?

192. Write about the first day of your current job. Has your initial opinions of things and people where you work changed since then?

193. Write about the last time you forgave someone for something. What was the original problem?

194. Write about an experience you have had with a bike. Were you riding the bike?

195. Write about three things that could be found in your search history that represent who you are.

196. Describe your first job. Did you enjoy it, and would you do it again if you could go back in time?

197. How important is it to meet a parent's expectations?

198. Write about a time that you saved up for something. Did it turn out to be worth it?

199. Write about a piece of technology that has become outdated during your lifetime. How did it work originally and what was it replaced with?

200. Write about the most memorable experience you have ordering takeout food. What specifically made it memorable?

201. Write about a time you got a haircut. Were you happy with the results? Why or why not?

202. Write about a time that you sold something. What did you sell and who did you sell it to?

203. Describe a game that you enjoy playing. How do you play and who do you typically play with?

204. Write about a time that you taught someone something.

205. Describe your largest insecurity as a teenager.
Looking back, was it worth being self-conscious about?

206. Is being famous a blessing or a curse? Explain why or
why not. Would you personally enjoy being famous?

207. Is it important to learn more than one language?
Explain a situation you have experienced where knowledge of
another language could have been useful.

208. Write about a time that you felt alone. How did this experience impact who you are today?

209. In detail, describe the room you are currently writing in. Paint a vivid picture of where you are.

210. Would you rather live in an apartment or a house? Explain your choice.

211. What is something that interests you. Describe how you were first introduced to it and what you know about it.

212. Write about a hobby you would like to take up but haven't yet found the time to.

213. Write about an activity that you used to do frequently but no longer partake in.

214. Write about an experience you have moving somewhere.
Describe how you felt leaving as well as starting to live
somewhere else.

215. Have you ever had a roommate or housemate? If so, describe your experience. If not, is it an experience you regret not having?

216. Write about a time that you applied for something. Did you get what you were applying for?

217. Write about a time that someone confided in you. How did it make you feel that they could trust you?

218. Write about a time you took the train somewhere. Describe your experience and where you were going.

219. Describe an experience you have had with a boat.

220. Write about your favorite childhood toy. Describe it
in detail.

221. How important is it to vote? How often do you vote?

222. Write about an experience you have swimming. If you cannot swim, is this a skill that you would one day like to learn and why?

223. Do you prefer going to the ocean or to the pool?

224. Write about something that you believed as a child that you eventually learned was not true. When and how did you find out the truth?

225. What is your biggest concern for the environment?

226. What is the future of artificial intelligence?

227. Describe a time that you got stuck in the rain.

228. What is your greatest weakness? Are you doing anything to improve upon it?

229. Have you ever collected something? If so, describe your collection. If not, what is something you would like to collect?

230. Describe a time that you've gotten lucky.

231. Write about a party that you've been to. Where was it and what was being celebrated?

232. Do you prefer taking a shower or taking a bath? Describe why.

233. Describe in detail the last time that you ate at a restaurant.

234. Write about a time that you felt uncomfortable.

235. Write detailed instructions on how to brush your teeth.

236. Write a letter to your future self about how you currently feel and what you aspire to become.

237. Write about a day that you were absent from school as a child.

238. Write about a memorable summer vacation when you were growing up.

239. Describe an injury that you have sustained. Do you still feel its effects in any ways?

240. Describe the last time that you felt surprised. Where were you and what were you doing?

----

241. Rewrite the end of your favorite movie or book. Describe what would happen in your alternative ending and why it should end like this.

----

242. Write about an experience you have with a
graduation ceremony.

243. Describe a specific smell that takes you back to
a specific memory.

244. Write about a current event that you remember watching unfold live. Describe where you were and who you were with.

245. Describe with detail a typical school lunch from your childhood.

246. Write about your ideal weather. Do you prefer the heat or the cold? What place have you been that best represents this climate.

247. Write about an experience you have had waiting in a line. Describe in detail how you felt and what you saw.

248. How important is organization to success? Write about ways that you organize different aspects of your life.

249. Write about something that people do in public that makes you feel uncomfortable.

250. Write about a place that you have driven past or through but have never stopped in physically. What was your impression of this place?

251. Describe a beautiful sunset or sunrise that you have seen. Where were you and how did it make you feel?

252. Has your opinion regarding a political issue ever changed or evolved? If so, describe what led to this evolution or change in your thinking. If not, explain why your ideas have remained so concrete.

253. Is it possible to change someone's political opinion through discussion and debate? Why or why not?

254. Write about a specific news story or article you have seen recently in which you have learned something new.

255. How important is it to stay up to date with local and large-scale news? How closely do you follow the news?

256. Write about a time that you did something charitable.
How did this make you feel, and would you do it again?

257. If you had the ability to go back in time to witness any live event in history, what would it be and why?

258. If you were a fruit, what would you be? Explain what specifically led you to this choice.

259. Describe your favorite city. What stuck out about it specifically?

260. Describe three things that can be currently found in your trash can.

261. Write about a significant academic decision you have made. What were your options and what was the outcome?

262. Write about an experience you have had with an amusement park.

263. Write about a time that technology failed you.

264. Create a schedule outlining your perfect day. Write small descriptions about each activity.

265. Compare yourself to someone you look up to.

266. Imagine you are designing a personal cologne or perfume. What would it be called and what would it smell like?

267. What is something that you have recently craved? Did you or did you not indulge your craving?

268. Pretend that you have accidently discovered a fossil. Describe what it looks like and come up with an original name for it.

269. Come up with an original ice cream flavor. Compare it to existing flavors and describe its taste.

270. Describe an invention that you think will replace texting and emailing.

271. Picture yourself in a maze. What does it look like, how do you feel and what is your initial plan of action?

272. Write about a time that you overestimated yourself. What were the implications of your overestimation?

273. Write about an experience you have involving fire.

274. There is an expression that states, "character is what you do when no one is watching." Write a new ending to this expression beginning "character is…"

275. Imagine you have just won a very prestigious award.
Write a short acceptance speech.

276. Write about an interaction that you have had with the police, (positive or negative). Describe how this situation made you feel.

277. Write about a time that you got away with something. What would have happened if you had gotten caught?

278. Write about an experience you have with peer
pressure. Looking back, would you have handled the
situation differently?

279. Imagine you have just landed on the moon. Describe
everything you see, feel, and think about.

280. If you could only eat one meal for the rest of your life, what would it be and why?

281. Come up with an idea for an app. What does it do? How would your life benefit from it if it existed?

282. Is marriage an essential part of life? Why or why not?

283. Write about a time that you made an unlikely
friendship. Are you still in contact with that person?

284. If you could choose to be athlete in any Olympic
sport, what would you choose?

285. Are horoscopes an accurate way to predict
a person's future? If so, are they something you
specifically refer to often? If not, why do you think
so many people believe in them?

286. Write about something taught to you in school as a
child that you now disagree with.

287. If you had to choose between the ability to fly and walk, which would you choose? Explain your reasoning.

288. Has there ever been a time in your life where you realized that what you were looking for had been right in front of you? When you realized, was it too late?

289. Write about a time that you have been in or around mountains. Describe them in detail.

290. There is an expression that states: "You can't judge a book by its cover." Do you feel as though this expression is accurate? Can there be exceptions?

291. Write about a situation where you were motivated to succeed by someone else's negative or positive expectations.

292. Write about something that exists today that you wish had existed when you were a child.

293. Describe your first-grade teacher. With detail, describe everything you can remember about him or her including what they looked like, how they dressed and how they spoke.

294. Write about a time that you studied for something.

295. Is a computer virus "alive"?

296. Imagine you are camping alone in the middle of the forest. Describe what your surroundings look like and how you feel. What are your thoughts as you prepare for sleeping outside?

297. Write about the last time that you laughed uncontrollably.

298. Imagine you are robbing a bank. Write out a comprehensive plan to how you would do it and who you would want to include.

299. Picture yourself on a desert island. Write about the three possessions and one person you would most want to be there with you.

300. Write about your most memorable Halloween.

301. Imagine you a professional wrestler. What would your name, backstory, outfit, and signature move be?

Inspiring | Educating | Creating | Entertaining

Brimming with creative inspiration, how-to projects, and useful information to enrich your everyday life, Quarto Knows is a favorite destination for those pursuing their interests and passions. Visit our site and dig deeper with our books into your area of interest: Quarto Creates, Quarto Cooks, Quarto Homes, Quarto Lives, Quarto Drives, Quarto Explores, Quarto Gifts, or Quarto Kids.

© 2020 by Quarto Publishing Group USA Inc.

First published in 2020 by Chartwell Books, an imprint of The Quarto Group, 142 West 36th Street, 4th Floor, New York, NY 10018, USA
T (212) 779-4972 F (212) 779-6058
www.QuartoKnows.com

Chartwell titles are also available at discount for retail, wholesale, promotional, and bulk purchase. For details, contact the Special Sales Manager by email at specialsales@quarto.com or by mail at The Quarto Group, Attn: Special Sales Manager, 100 Cummings Center Suite 265D, Beverly, MA 01915 USA.

10 9 8 7 6 5 4 3 2 1

ISBN: 978-0-7858-3906-4

Publisher: Rage Kindelsperger
Creative Director: Laura Drew
Managing Editor: Cara Donaldson
Text: Avi Z. Stern
Cover Design: Laura Drew
Interior Design: B. Middleworth

Printed in China